The Story of

NITROGEN

Karen Fitzgerald

A FIRST BOOK

Franklin Watts
A Division of Grolier Publishing
New York London Hong Kong Sydney
Danbury, Connecticut

To Jill and John

Chemical consultant: Geoffrey Buckwalter, Ph.D.

Cover and interior design by Robin Hessel Hoffmann

Photographs ©: BMCS (EOD) Leonard Sayles: 49; Comstock: 51; Corbis-Bettmann: 17, 45, 47; Edgar Fahs Smith Collection , Department of Special Collections, Van Pelt-Dietrich Library, University of Pennyslvania: 12; Fundamental Photos: cover bottom left (Kristen Brochmann), 39 (Richard Megna); North Wind Picture Archives: 18, 21, 26; Photo Researchers: 35 (Dr. Jeremy Burgess/SPL), 23 (Keith Kent/SPL), 7 (Richard Megna), 36 (Huge Spencer), 10 (Vanessa Vick), cover top right, 14 (Charles D. Winters); Superstock, Inc.: 54; Tom Pantages: 25, 38, 42.

Illustration by Lloyd Birmingham

Library of Congress Cataloging-in-Publication Data

Fitzgerald, Karen.
  The story of nitrogen / by Karen Fitzgerald
  p.   cm. — (A First book)
  Includes bibliographical references and index.
  Summary: Explores the history of the chemical element nitrogen and explains its chemistry, how it is used in industry, and its importance in our lives.
  ISBN 0-531-20248-8
  1. Nitrogen—Juvenile literature. [1. Nitrogen.] I. Title. II. Series.
QD181.N1F5 1997
546'.711—dc20   96-25876
                                                                 CIP   AC

Contents

Chapter 1

THE SHY GAS

Everybody has heard of oxygen. It's the invisible *gas* we must breathe to stay alive. Oxygen attracts a lot of attention, not only because it is so important to life but because it makes fire burn. But oxygen is just one of many gases in the air, and it is not even the most abundant one. A gas called *nitrogen* is the main ingredient of the air we breathe. Even though air has four times more nitrogen than oxygen, very few people know anything at all about nitrogen.

Nitrogen is like a shy guy at a party. While oxygen dazzles everyone with fire, nitrogen stays in the background, avoiding other substances as much as possible. So oxygen gets all the glory. But if people would just take the time to get to know nitrogen, they would find that it is also capable of fantastic things.

Billions of years ago, long before there was any oxygen in the air, volcanoes began spewing out tons of nitrogen. Thanks to these volcanoes, a blanket of nitrogen formed around the earth to nourish all living things.

Before it can contribute to life, though, nitrogen must be convinced to come out of its shell and bond with oxygen. Lightning is one thing that can force nitrogen and oxygen to combine and form gases known as *nitrogen oxides*. These nitrogen oxides can be washed out of the air by rain and carried to the ground.

Plants then absorb the nitrogen oxides and use the nitrogen to produce the proteins that enable stems and leaves to grow. Animals eat the plants and use the energy to build and maintain their own bodies. So you see, when the shy gas does bond with others, it becomes very important to life. At the end of life, nitrogen returns to the air through the process of decay.

After nitrogen bonds with oxygen, it is no longer a wallflower. Not only can it give plants important nutrients, but it can make fireworks too! The fireworks you see on the Fourth of July are the result of an explosive breakup between nitrogen and oxygen. Nitrogen is also the most important ingredient in many explosives, including *TNT*.

Even though nitrogen has been in the air for billions of years, scientists discovered it only 200 years ago. Since that time they have come to know this shy gas very well.

Nitrogen helps produce the beautiful explosions of fireworks.

They have learned why it likes to keep to itself and why it changes so strikingly when it bonds with other substances.

If you read on, you can get to know nitrogen too. You will discover that nitrogen does many wonderful things for us and our planet. But you will also find that its explosive nature has caused a great deal of destruction and death. You will learn what scientists know about nitrogen and all the ways it affects our lives. This is the story of nitrogen.

Chapter 2

DISCOVERING NITROGEN

Because nitrogen is so shy, it took a while for people to notice it exists. People found nitrogen combined with other substances in compounds long before they discovered pure nitrogen gas. One of the first nitrogen compounds to be discovered was a substance that forms in piles of animal manure. It looks like little crystals, or large grains of salt, so it is called *saltpeter*, but it is also known as *niter*.

The Chinese began experimenting with niter more than 1,000 years ago. Back then, they tried mixing many different substances together to find a medicine that could make people live forever. These early chemists believed this medicine would also help them make gold. One day

During the Chinese New Year, the streets of Chinatown in New York City are covered with exploded firecrackers.

they discovered something quite amazing when they mixed it with charcoal and a yellow powder called sulfur. If they set it on fire, it exploded! They got the bright idea to make firecrackers from this mixture. Today, Chinese people still celebrate their New Year by setting off firecrackers made of the same ingredients.

No one could have guessed back then that saltpeter contains nitrogen. They didn't even know nitrogen was in the air. The first person to realize that air contains more than one gas may have been a Chinese man named Mao-Khoa. In the 700s, he wrote that air is made of what he called yin and yang. He described yang as perfect by itself because it did not interact with other things. It sounds a lot like nitrogen. Yin, he said, was an incomplete sort of air that was sucked into burning materials. Oxygen is indeed drawn into a flame.

If this story is true, Mao-Khoa's findings never reached Europe. For until the 1700s, Europeans believed that air was an *element*, a basic substance that could not be broken down into different parts. They believed that earth, air, fire, and water were the four elements that made up everything in the world.

THE GUNPOWDER EXPLOSION

While European scientists remained unaware of the two parts of air, they certainly heard about the Chinese firecracker powder. In the 900s, the Chinese had begun using

火籠箭式

One of the first uses of gunpowder was for launching
fiery arrows against enemies in China.

it to launch fiery arrows against enemies during battle. After they invented cannons and guns that worked by exploding the black powder, the knowledge of the niter mixture quickly spread to the Middle East and then to Europe. By the 1400s, this gunpowder changed the way wars were fought in Europe. Arrows and spears became a thing of the past.

Niter also had another valuable—but very different—use. When added to soil, it made crops grow larger and more quickly. During the Middle Ages, Europeans experimented with niter quite a bit to learn more about its unusual powers.

A Swiss physician named Paracelsus noticed that an explosion of gunpowder is a lot like lightning and thunder. As a result, in the 1600s, scientists began to believe that lightning and thunder are caused by the collision of sulfur particles and niter particles in the air. Some people believed that particles of niter also made vegetables grow. Although these ideas were wrong, scientists were beginning to realize that the air contains particles of different substances.

Scientists burned niter with sulfur and collected the fumes that rose into the air. By condensing the fumes into a liquid, the scientists formed a very powerful substance called *nitric acid*. When they poured nitric acid on a metal such as copper, smoke fizzled up into the air. The *acid* rapidly dissolved the metal, leaving a powder behind. This is a chemical reaction in which the metal changes into something else.

Nitric acid eats through a strip of copper.

DIFFERENT KINDS OF AIR

In the early 1700s, an English doctor named Stephen Hales became fascinated by the smoky fumes given off by various chemical reactions. They were gases, but Hales thought they were air that had somehow become trapped in solids or liquids. To see how much "air" each reaction produced, he began collecting it in bottles. Hales was amazed to find that the reaction between nitric acid and iron produced a large quantity of "air." And the explosion of niter generated even more fumes in a very short time. It was all this gas that gave the explosion its destructive power.

Hales also collected the gases that rose from burning substances. He did not check for differences among the gases because, like most other scientists of his time, he assumed they were all just air. But he knew that a flame would not light in the air remaining after a candle had burned in a small space. Hales explained it by suggesting that the air had somehow become "infected." Today we know the flame would not light because the candle had used up all the oxygen.

Hales's "air," of course, was nitrogen. Soon chemists began to notice other differences in the gases that came out of solid materials. But nitrogen was often confused with *carbon dioxide* because a flame cannot burn in either of them. Sometime around 1770, an English chemist named Henry Cavendish discovered a difference between the two. When carbon dioxide was passed through lye, a

15

substance used to make soap, the "air" was absorbed. But the lye did not absorb nitrogen.

After hearing about his experiments, a fellow chemist named Joseph Priestley remarked that no substance seemed able to absorb the gas remaining after a flame burned in air. While other gases would dissolve in water, this one did not. In fact, everything that was known to absorb gases had been tried, but nothing affected this strange "air."

Unfortunately, Cavendish did not publish the results of his tests for all the world to see. So two other chemists got credit for discovering nitrogen. One of them was a Scottish chemist, Daniel Rutherford, who distinguished nitrogen from carbon dioxide in the same way Cavendish did. Rutherford didn't know it, but about that time, Carl Wilhelm Scheele, a Swedish chemist, did some other tests showing the same thing. They both published their results in 1772.

Scheele was the first person to give the new gas a name. Because fire and animals could not live in it, he called it *foul air*, or rotten air. He discovered that it makes up about 80 percent of the air around us. The rest was a substance that fire thrived in, so he called it *fire air*. Of course, it was oxygen.

It was not long before a French chemist named Antoine Lavoisier discovered that fire is a *chemical reaction* in which oxygen combines with wood, or whatever is burning. Fire, he realized, is not an element at all. And since air contains at least two substances, it could not be

One of the discoverers of nitrogen,
Carl Wilhelm Scheele, called it "foul air."

Antoine Lavoisier was the first to recognize nitrogen as an element.

an element either. By this time, more than one substance had already been discovered in "earth." The four-element theory was crumbling. Lavoisier finally put an end to it when he discovered that water is made of hydrogen and oxygen.

In 1789, Lavoisier announced that the real elements numbered more than thirty. Oxygen and hydrogen were among these elements, and so was nitrogen. Lavoisier called nitrogen *azote*, which means "no life" in Greek, and it is still called azote in France.

Some experiments done by Cavendish inspired its English name. The experiments showed for the first time that nitric acid and niter contain nitrogen. After hearing about them, a French chemist named Jean-Antoine Chaptal suggested that "foul air" be called nitrogen, which means "generator of niter."

Nitrogen was getting some attention. At last, Lavoisier considered nitrogen to be one of five elements that are special because they are so common in our world. Not only is nitrogen a major part of the air, but it is in niter, nitric acid, and ammonia. Lavoisier's discoveries set scientists on the road to modern chemistry and soon, chemists discovered many more nitrogen *compounds*. As you will find in the next chapter, the great variety of these compounds helped chemists solve the mystery of why elements join together.

Chapter 3

UNCOMMON BONDS

After Lavoisier's chemical revolution revealed nitrogen to the world, chemists began getting to know the shy gas better. They found that although it doesn't have much of a personality, it is capable of fantastic things when it joins forces with others.

For a loner, nitrogen forms a remarkable variety of compounds. The bonds it makes with oxygen alone were enough to help chemists figure out what elements are made of and how they form compounds. It all started when an Englishman named John Dalton became interested in the weather.

Dalton grew up among the mountains and lakes of England, where the weather changed rapidly. To help

*John Dalton discovered what elements
are made of by studying the air.*

farmers predict the weather, he started measuring the amount of water in the air in different places. He thought these measurements might show when it was about to rain.

When he saw how much the amount of water changed from day to day, he realized something very important about the air. He envisioned particles of water spreading through the spaces between particles of air. As more water evaporates into the air, he guessed, the water particles simply move into whatever empty space is available.

At the time—the early 1800s—nearly all scientists thought water particles were attached to air particles in a compound. But Dalton realized that the particles simply mix together. Eventually he came to understand that air is a mixture of nitrogen, oxygen, carbon dioxide, and other gases. These gas particles are not attached to each other, but are free to move around each other like fish in a crowded lake.

Dalton experimented with many different gases including nitrogen and oxygen. After comparing how well the gases dissolved in water, he began to suspect that they were made of tiny particles whose size and weight varied from element to element. These particles, called *atoms*, were the smallest units of each element.

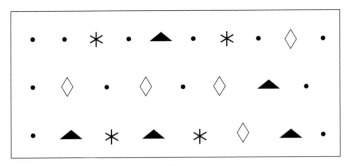

John Dalton drew this picture to show how particles of different gases mix in the air: the dots are nitrogen, the diamonds are oxygen, the black triangles are carbon dioxide, and the stars are water vapor.

NITROGEN OXIDE CLUES

Dalton also studied gases that were compounds of nitrogen and oxygen—the nitrogen oxides. He knew there were several different nitrogen oxides. One of them, *nitric oxide*, forms when an electric spark is added to a mixture of nitrogen and oxygen. This same reaction occurs when a lightning bolt travels through the air during a thunderstorm.

A bolt of lightning brings nitrogen and oxygen together to form nitric oxide.

Dalton compared the amounts of nitrogen and oxygen in three nitrogen oxide gases and saw an amazing pattern. One gas had twice as much oxygen as another, and the third gas had four times as much oxygen as the first. He realized that this strange doubling came about because the number of oxygen atoms per nitrogen atom doubled from one gas to the next. That meant that the oxygen and nitrogen atoms were attached to one another in little groups that were repeated throughout each gas.

Today scientists know that nitric oxide is made of one oxygen atom attached to each nitrogen atom. A second nitrogen oxide compound, which takes the form of a reddish-brown gas, contains two oxygen atoms for every nitrogen atom. This substance is called *nitrogen dioxide*. A third gas, *nitrous oxide*, has two nitrogen atoms attached to each oxygen atom.

So you see, the nitrogen oxide gases helped Dalton realize that elements are made of atoms. His atomic theory allowed scientists to understand what happens during chemical reactions.

When elements react chemically, their atoms attach to each other in groups called *molecules*. Each compound can be identified by the special combination of atoms in its molecules. Chemists represent nitric oxide, for instance, by the formula NO. N represents a nitrogen atom and O represents an oxygen atom.

Mixing nitric oxide with oxygen adds another atom to each molecule, producing nitrogen dioxide. Its formula

The brown gas that rises when nitric acid reacts with copper is nitrogen dioxide.

is NO_2. When nitrogen dioxide dissolves in water, it forms nitric acid. Hydrogen and oxygen atoms in the water combine with nitrogen dioxide to create HNO_3, or nitric acid.

When nitric acid is poured on certain metals, nitrous oxide is given off. It has a formula of N_2O. In 1801, a chemist named Humphry Davy tried inhaling this gas and found that it had a strange effect. He began to feel happy

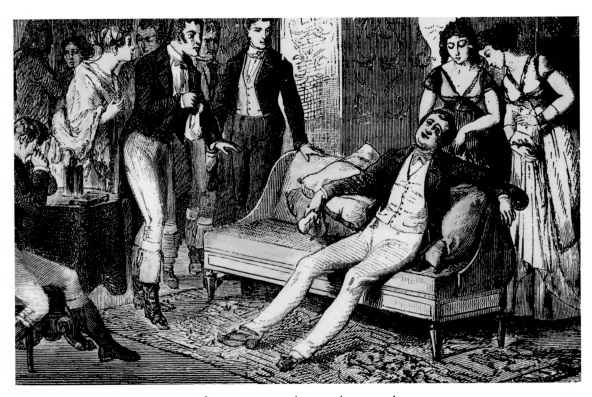

After nitrous oxide was discovered,
some people tried inhaling it at parties.

and giggly. Today nitrous oxide is informally known as "laughing gas," but it can also relieve physical pain. Some dentists give their patients laughing gas for that reason.

As you can see, the combination of nitrogen and oxygen produces some interesting results. These compounds have much more unusual personalities than nitrogen alone. Nitric oxide and nitrogen dioxide are poisonous, and nitric acid is a very powerful acid. In fact, it is the only acid that can separate silver from gold.

THE ODD COUPLE

In all, there are at least seven nitrogen oxides. Many of them are harmful because they react with other substances very easily. Why is nitrogen so much more reactive when it is in a compound? It has to do with the way nitrogen combines with other atoms.

Every atom contains tiny particles called *electrons*. These electrons move around the center, or *nucleus*, of the atom and form bonds with other atoms. A nitrogen atom has seven electrons—two are close to the nucleus and the remaining five are farther away, on the outside of the atom.

Electrons usually gather in groups of two or eight. The outside group of five electrons needs three more electrons to complete its group, so nitrogen atoms bond with atoms that have three electrons to spare. A *hydrogen* atom has one lonely electron that is always looking to join the electrons of other atoms. If three hydrogen atoms bond with one nitrogen atom, the electrons of all four atoms are satisfied. The resulting compound, NH_3, is ammonia.

Oxygen has one more electron than nitrogen, so it has six electrons in its outer group. It looks for atoms that

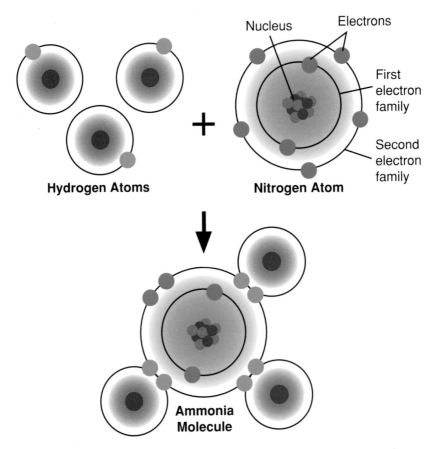

A nitrogen atom bonds with three hydrogen atoms to get eight electrons in its outer shell. The result is ammonia.

have two electrons to spare, so it often bonds with two hydrogen atoms to form water, H_2O.

But nitrogen and oxygen make an odd couple. Their outer families of electrons don't fit together very well. That is part of the reason why nitrogen resists bonding with oxygen in the air. Another reason is that nitrogen atoms in the air are already happily bonded to each other.

Pure nitrogen gas has a formula of N_2. In this pair, the atoms are attached by a triple bond. Each atom shares three of its outer electrons with the other atom. This gives each atom a complete family of eight electrons. The triple bond makes the nitrogen molecule very stable, so it doesn't interact much with other elements.

Oxygen atoms in the air also bond in pairs, with each atom sharing two electrons. This *double bond* is not very satisfying, however. If given the chance, oxygen almost always prefers bonding with another element.

A FORCED MARRIAGE

It takes a lot of energy to convince nitrogen to bond with oxygen. Heat and fire can't do it, but electricity can. Even when nitrogen and oxygen do bond, nitrogen doesn't seem very happy. In nitric oxide, for instance, the oxygen atom shares only two electrons with nitrogen. This means that nitrogen has seven electrons in its outer family. Since nitrogen would like eight electrons, it is not completely satisfied. To get out of this unhappy situation, nitric oxide reacts easily with other substances.

Periodic Table

1 **H** 1.00794 Hydrogen	

3 **Li** 6.941 Lithium	**4** **Be** 9.01218 Beryllium

11 **Na** 22.98977 Sodium	**12** **Mg** 24.305 Magnesium

19 **K** 39.0983 Potassium	**20** **Ca** 40.078 Calcium	**21** **Sc** 44.95591 Scandium	**22** **Ti** 47.88 Titanium	**23** **V** 50.9415 Vanadium	**24** **Cr** 51.9161 Chromium	**25** **Mn** 54.93805 Manganese	**26** **Fe** 55.847 Iron	**27** **Co** 58.9332 Cobalt
37 **Rb** 85.4678 Rubidium	**38** **Sr** 87.62 Strontium	**39** **Y** 88.9059 Yttrium	**40** **Zr** 91.224 Zirconium	**41** **Nb** 92.9064 Niobium	**42** **Mo** 95.94 Molybdenum	**43** **Tc** (98) Technetium	**44** **Ru** 101.07 Ruthenium	**45** **Rh** 102.9055 Rhodium
55 **Cs** 132.9054 Cesium	**56** **Ba** 137.327 Barium	**57** **La** * 138.9055 Lanthanum	**72** **Hf** 178.49 Hafnium	**73** **Ta** 180.9479 Tantalum	**74** **W** 183.85 Tungsten	**75** **Re** 186.207 Rhenium	**76** **Os** 190.2 Osmium	**77** **Ir** 192.22 Iridium
87 **Fr** (223) Francium	**88** **Ra** 226.025 Radium	**89** **Ac** ** (227) Actinium	**104** **Unq** (261)† (Unnilquadium)	**105** **Unp** (262)† (Unnilpentium)	**106** **Unh** (263)† (Unnilhoxium)	**107** **Uns** (262)† (Unnilseptium)	**108** **Uno** (265)† (Unniloctium)	**109** **Une** (266)† (Unnilnonium)

Scientists find it helpful to organize elements in a chart called the periodic table of the elements. An element's position in the table is determined by its atomic number. Because an atom of nitrogen has seven protons, its atomic number is 7.

58 **Ce** 140.115 Cerium	**59** **Pr** 140.9077 Praseodymium	**60** **Nd** 144.24 Neodymium	**61** **Pm** (145) Promethium	**62** **Sm** 150.36 Samarium
90 **Th** 232.0381 Thorium	**91** **Pa** 231.0359 Protactinium	**92** **U** 238.029 Uranium	**93** **Np** 237.048 Neptunium	**94** **Pu** (244) Plutonium

of the Elements

CHEMICAL SYMBOL · ATOMIC NUMBER

ATOMIC WEIGHT

ELEMENT NAME

						2 **He** 4.00260 Helium
5 **B** 10.811 Boron	6 **C** 12.011 Carbon	7 **N** 14.067 Nitrogen	8 **O** 15.994 Oxygen	9 **F** 18.998403 Florine	10 **Ne** 20.1797 Neon
13 **Al** 26.96154 Aluminum	14 **Si** 28.0855 Silicon	15 **P** 30.973762 Phosphorous	16 **S** 32.066 Sulfur	17 **Cl** 35.4527 Chlorine	18 **Ar** 39.948 Argon

28 **Ni** 58.693 Nickel	29 **Cu** 63.546 copper	30 **Zn** 65.39 Zinc	31 **Ga** 69.723 Gallium	32 **Ge** 72.61 Germanium	33 **As** 72.9216 Arsenic	34 **Se** 78.96 Selenium	35 **Br** 79.904 Bromine	36 **Kr** 83.80 Krypton
46 **Pd** 106.42 Palladium	47 **Ag** 107.8682 Silver	48 **Cd** 112.41 Cadmium	49 **In** 114.82 Indium	50 **Sn** 118.71 Tin	51 **Sb** 121.757 Antimony	52 **Te** 127.60 Tellurium	53 **I** 126.9045 Iodine	54 **Xe** 131.29 Xenon
78 **Pt** 195.08 Platinum	79 **Au** 196.9665 Gold	80 **Hg** 200.59 Mercury	81 **Ti** 204.383 Thallium	82 **Pb** 207.2 Lead	83 **Bi** 208.9804 Bismuth	84 **Po** (209) Polonium	85 **At** (210) Astatine	86 **Rn** (222) Radon

63 **Eu** 151.965 Europium	64 **Gd** 157.25 Gadolinium	65 **Tb** 158.9253 Terbium	66 **Dy** 162.50 Dysprosium	67 **Ho** 164.9303 Holmium	68 **Er** 167.26 Erbium	69 **Tm** 168.9342 Thulium	70 **Yb** 173.04 Ytterbium	71 **Lu** 174.967 Lutetium

95 **Am** (243) Americium	96 **Cm** (247) Berkelium	97 **Bk** (247) Berkelium	98 **Cf** (251) Californium	99 **Es** (252) Einsteinium	100 **Fm** (257) Fermium	101 **Md** (258) Mendelevium	102 **No** (259) Nobelium	103 **Lr** (260) Lawrencium

Even when another oxygen atom joins a nitric oxide molecule, making nitrogen dioxide, nitrogen is still not satisfied. Nitrogen is looking for just one more electron, but the new oxygen atom insists on sharing two electrons to complete its own family of electrons.

In nitric acid, HNO_3, hydrogen and nitrogen each share an electron with one of the oxygen atoms. Each of the other two oxygen atoms makes a strange connection called a coordinate bond with the nitrogen atom. Because it has two *coordinate bonds*, nitric acid reacts easily with other substances, such as metals.

Rain dissolves nitrogen dioxide in the air and carries it to the ground as nitric acid. There, it sometimes reacts with a metal called *potassium*. This metal has one atom in its outer ring. A potassium atom can replace the hydrogen atom in nitric acid, and potassium nitrate is born. Its formula is KNO_3. This compound is none other than niter, the explosive fertilizer discovered in ancient times.

Nitrogen, you may have noticed, has trouble making lasting friendships. Its relationship with oxygen can be especially rocky—even explosive. But, as you will find in the next chapter, nitrogen's relationships with other elements can give birth to life.

Chapter 4

A MATTER OF LIFE AND DEATH

Nitrogen is happy floating around in the air, above all earthly problems and concerns. It is in a stable relationship with another atom just like itself. But every once in a while, something such as lightning forces a nitrogen couple to split up.

When that happens, the atoms come down to Earth and take part in the great cycle of life and death known as the *nitrogen cycle*. In this cycle, nitrogen helps create plants and animals. Then, when the plants and animals die and decay, nitrogen returns to its safe haven in the air.

In 1862, scientists realized that plants and animals cannot get the nitrogen they need from the air. The reason is that they are not able to break the strong *triple bonds* that hold nitrogen molecules together. Even though a plant may be in desperate need of nitrogen, the nitrogen molecules in the air wander blissfully about in the breeze. Similarly, when an animal inhales nitrogen molecules, they turn right around and leave the animal's lungs the next time it exhales.

Since pure nitrogen does not dissolve in water, even rain cannot bring it down to Earth. Lightning is powerful enough to break up the molecules, but it doesn't hit nitrogen molecules that often. And although sunlight of high energy can split them up, not many high-energy rays reach the part of the atmosphere that contains nitrogen molecules.

Fortunately, there are creatures in the soil—called bacteria—that can split nitrogen molecules. These tiny bacteria have only one cell, yet they are strong enough to break the triple bond! Once the nitrogen atoms are single, they become part of compounds that can dissolve in water. When plants absorb the water through their roots, they can process the nitrogen and use it to build the compounds they need to live.

In a way, the bacteria hold, or fix, the nitrogen in place, since it is no longer able to float freely in the air. Scientists call the service bacteria perform *nitrogen fixation*. Whenever its triple bond is broken, nitrogen is said to be fixed.

Some kinds of bacteria actually move into the root hairs of plants, such as peas and soybeans. They give the plant a constant supply of nitrogen, and in return the plant

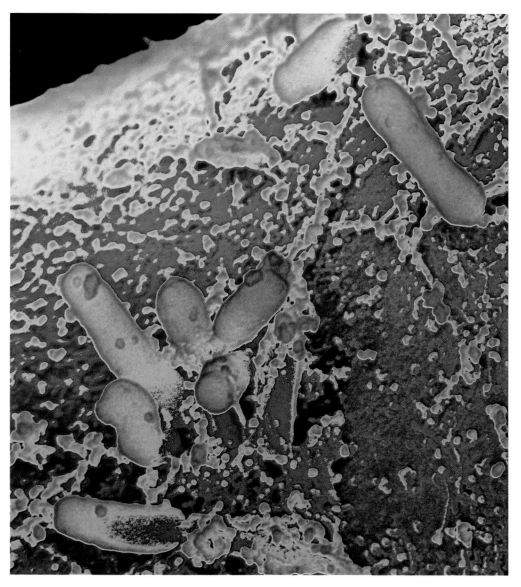

These nitrogen-fixing bacteria (colored orange and magnified thousands of times) are inside a root hair of a pea plant.

gives them the compounds they need to do their jobs. The plant creates a little bump, called a *root nodule*, around colonies of these bacteria.

Communities of nitrogen-fixing bacteria live in bumps on the roots of pea plants and other legumes.

In the ocean, blue-green algae fix nitrogen for underwater plants. So you see, bacteria and algae perform a great service for plants. Even today, scientists haven't quite figured out how they break the triple nitrogen bond.

PLANT OFFERINGS

Some nitrogen-fixing bacteria change nitrogen to ammonia. Others make *nitrates*, which are compounds with NO_3 in their formulas. Plants can use either ammonia or nitrates to make the compounds they need.

The compounds usually consist of a chain or ring of carbon atoms with NH_2 groups attached here and there. Because an NH_2 group, is similar to ammonia, NH_3, it is called the *amine group*. Complex compounds containing one or more amine groups are called *amino acids*. Amino acids link together to form even more complicated spiral molecules. These molecules are *proteins*, which plants use to build stems and leaves.

When people and other animals eat plants, they use the plant proteins to build the proteins their bodies need. Long, stringy proteins are used to make hair, skin, muscles, and other body parts. Unusually shaped proteins called *enzymes* keep the body running properly.

Proteins contain many different elements—carbon, hydrogen, oxygen, and sometimes sulfur—but they would not be proteins without nitrogen. It is the amine groups in amino acids that make proteins unique. About 16 percent

A molecule of troponin, found in muscle, is, like all proteins, very complex. Nitrogen atoms are blue in this computer model.

of all proteins is nitrogen. The genes that determine our inherited traits also contain nitrogen, in the substance known as DNA. Nitrogen, you see, helps make the amazing complexity of human beings possible.

THE END OF LIFE

When proteins are no longer useful, the body breaks them down into simpler compounds and replaces them with new proteins. The simpler compounds then become part of the waste that people and animals eliminate from their bodies every day.

One of the simplest of these nitrogen compounds is called *urea*. Its name comes from urine, the liquid that carries urea out of our bodies. Urea and other waste compounds in manure contain amine groups. Like ammonia, these compounds tend to have awful smells.

This is a close-up of crystals of urea, a nitrogen compound in urine.

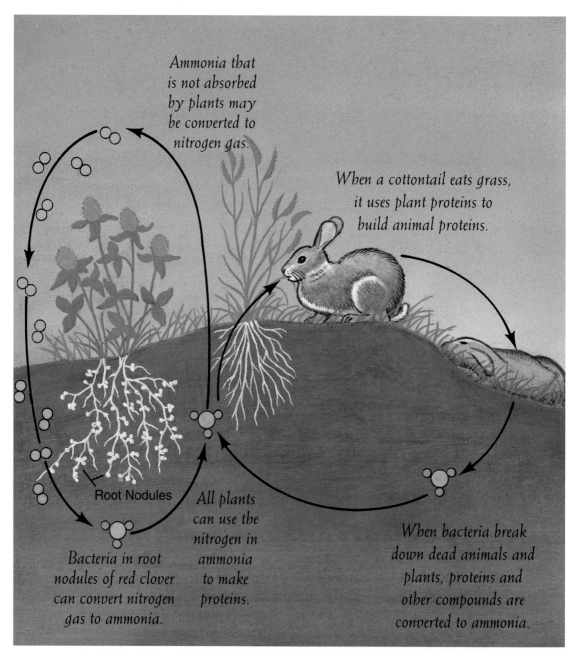

Ammonia that
is not absorbed
by plants may
be converted to
nitrogen gas.

When a cottontail eats grass,
it uses plant proteins to
build animal proteins.

Root Nodules

All plants
can use the
nitrogen in
ammonia
to make
proteins.

Bacteria in root
nodules of red clover
can convert nitrogen
gas to ammonia.

When bacteria break
down dead animals and
plants, proteins and
other compounds are
converted to ammonia.

Plants need nitrogen to grow, but they cannot break down nitrogen
gas. This diagram shows how nitrogen travels through an ecosystem.

When plants and animals die, bacteria break proteins down into other smelly compounds. This decay process eventually produces ammonia. It is a good thing decay compounds smell bad because the smell keeps us away from bacteria that can make us sick.

If the ammonia is not taken up again to fertilize plants, it may rise into the air as a gas. The nitrogen atom eventually separates from the hydrogen atoms and, once again, becomes half of a nitrogen couple.

So at the end of an organism's life, nitrogen returns to its little heaven in the air. Reunited with a perfectly compatible companion, it settles into a peaceful existence.

When nitrogen comes to down to Earth, it actively participates in the world, creating plants and animals. Coming into contact with elements so different from itself seems to inspire nitrogen to do fantastic and ingenious things. Although nitrogen makes up less than 3 percent of the weight of the human body, its compounds are largely responsible for our intelligence and most of our bodies' functions.

The power of nitrogen is revealed in all its glory in living things. In the next chapter, you will see how fireworks and explosives display the power of nitrogen in a different way.

Nitrogen compounds are still a major component of most explosives.
This quarry is being blasted with ammonium nitrate.

Chapter 5

THE NITROGEN EXPLOSION

It is hard to believe that something as creative as nitrogen could be destructive too. But like many creative geniuses, nitrogen seems to have a temper. It's as if leaving its airy home and uniting with oxygen puts the shy gas on edge. At the slightest insult, nitrogen can blow up and return to the atmosphere.

It's not surprising that one of the first nitrogen compounds that attracted the attention of ancient chemists was an explosive—niter. Every Fourth of July we see that nitrogen can put on a display that goes far beyond the flames oxygen creates. Fireworks have advanced quite a bit since the Chinese invented them, but niter is still an important ingredient. Gunpowder propels fireworks into the sky and bursts them open, releasing light and color. This powder is about 75 percent niter, 15 percent *carbon*, and 10 percent sulfur. That's about the same mixture the Chinese used a thousand years ago.

The first guns were powered with black powder. Soldiers poured it into their gun barrels and pounded it until it was packed very hard. After sliding in a round bullet, the soldier pulled the trigger. This created a spark that set off the gun powder, and the explosion fired the bullet forward.

Why does gunpowder explode? The uneasy relationship between the nitrogen and oxygen atoms in the niter is the key. Igniting gunpowder gives the oxygen atoms the opportunity to leave nitrogen and bond with nearby carbon or sulfur atoms. Since oxygen and nitrogen don't get along all that well, oxygen jumps at the chance.

The gases carbon dioxide, CO_2, and sulfur dioxide, SO_2, form as a result. The nitrogen atoms, freed from the niter, reunite with each other. Whenever atoms bond, they generate heat. All the new bonds being formed create so much heat in such a short period of time that there is an explosion. It is the only way to quickly get rid of all the heat. In addition, there are so many hot gases shooting out of the gunpowder that the surrounding air goes into shock. A powerful shock wave rushes outward, creating a loud boom.

A nitrogen explosive much more powerful than niter was discovered in 1846. It is *nitroglycerin*, a liquid compound containing nitrate groups (NO_3), carbon, and

During the Revolutionary War, soldiers filled their guns with gunpowder from powder horns.

hydrogen. When nitroglycerin explodes, the nitrogen and oxygen in the nitrate groups split up, and the oxygen combines with nearby carbon and hydrogen atoms. Superhot carbon dioxide, water vapor, and nitrogen blast outward, destroying everything in their path.

Nitroglycerin is so powerful because it has three nitrate groups in each molecule instead of one. As a result, more new bonds are created, generating more heat and gases. Another reason is that the carbon and hydrogen atoms are closer to the oxygen atoms in the nitroglycerin molecule than in the gunpowder mixture.

Nitroglycerin is so sensitive that it can blow up at the slightest disturbance. Just hitting it or dropping it can set if off. Amazingly enough, nitroglycerin can help people with heart disease too. When these people have chest pains, they take pills containing a very tiny amount of nitroglycerin. The nitroglycerin relaxes the vessels that deliver blood to the heart, preventing a heart attack.

AN EXPLODING INDUSTRY

Because nitroglycerin can explode so easily, it was difficult to find a way to manufacture it safely. Many people died trying, including the brother of a Swedish chemist named Alfred Nobel. In 1865, a year after his brother died, Nobel found a way to produce nitroglycerin safely. A short time later, Nobel invented an even safer explosive called *dynamite*. Dynamite is nitroglycerin that has been absorbed in a solid

Alfred Nobel found a way to safely produce nitrogen explosives.

material that holds the sensitive liquid in place. Later, to further improve the safety of dynamite, Nobel began mixing it with a chemical called ammonium nitrate, NH_4NO_3. Although ammonium nitrate is not as powerful as dynamite, it is less expensive to manufacture and easier to use.

Nobel hoped that his products would be used for only peaceful purposes such as blasting holes through rock to make way for roads and tunnels or creating mines and oil wells. To encourage peace, in general, Nobel set aside money for the Nobel Prizes. Each year, they are awarded to people who make great contributions to peace, literature, and science.

Ammonium nitrate is still one of the most widely used explosives. It is also a very popular fertilizer; only pure ammonia fertilizes plants better. In 1995, the widespread availability of ammonium nitrate fertilizer led to a horrible tragedy. Some of this fertilizer was used to build a bomb that blew up a United States government building in Oklahoma City.

The most powerful nitrogen-based explosive, TNT, was first used by the military in World War I. It is still the most important chemical explosive used by the military. The letters TNT stand for the explosive's chemical name—trinitrotoluene. *Tri-* indicates that one TNT molecule has three nitro groups. Each nitro group contains one nitrogen and two oxygen atoms. The nitro groups are attached to toluene, which is a ring of carbon and hydrogen atoms. TNT works like nitroglycerin, but is more powerful because the atoms are closer together.

Nitrogen is the main ingredient of many powerful explosives. In this military exercise, soldiers are using TNT to blow up a van.

NITROGEN AT WORK

Nitrogen compounds have other uses that have nothing to do with explosives. As you already know, the most important of these invloves the production of fertilizer. But there are other uses too. Silk, nylon, and many dyes contain nitrogen. Other nitrogen compounds are important medicines such as antibiotics, which kill bacteria, and antihistamines, which relieve allergy symptoms. Some are drugs that affect the way people feel by interfering with the working of the brain. These drugs include caffeine, cocaine, and heroin. Still other nitrogen compounds are poisonous. Two of them, cyanide and strychnine, are powerful enough to kill people. Here again, we see the two sides of nitrogen; combined with some elements, it can restore health, but in other combinations, it can kill.

The first plastic was a nitrate called celluloid. Although it was once used in motion-picture film, it has been replaced because it catches fire easily. Other nitrates are used in making meat products such as hot dogs, bacon, salami, and bologna.

Industries use many nitrogen compounds, such as nitric acid, to produce other substances. Nitrogen gas is also important in industry. That may seem strange since it doesn't usually react with anything, but industries use it for that very reason. Placing materials in pure nitrogen protects them from attack by oxygen and water, which can *corrode* materials by reacting chemically with them. Nitrogen acts as a blanket over the materials to keep everything else out.

*A California sugar beet farmer fertilizes the soil
by injecting it with liquid ammonia.*

Most importantly, nitrogen gas is used to make ammonia and other compounds. It took scientists many years to figure out how to make ammonia. Even though there is plenty of nitrogen in the air, people could not figure out how to make it bond with hydrogen. Scientists were unable to do what bacteria do all the time—fix nitrogen.

Toward the end of the 1800s, demand for fertilizers and explosives increased. Finding a way to fix nitrogen became more important than ever. Electricity could have been used to force nitrogen and oxygen to bond, but it would have cost too much to do it on a regular basis.

Finally in 1909, a German chemist named Fritz Haber discovered that combining nitrogen and hydrogen under high pressure and temperatures did the trick. A substance called a *catalyst* also had to be added to help the reaction take place. It is so difficult for people to fix nitrogen, it is amazing that tiny bacteria can do it so easily.

FIXING THE NITROGEN CYCLE

Today, companies that manufacture explosives and fertilizers fix huge quantities of nitrogen. Unfortunately, all this nitrogen-fixing has upset the nitrogen cycle. Twice as much nitrogen now comes to Earth as returns to the atmosphere.

More nitrogen on the ground might sound like a good thing because it makes plants grow better. But too much growth can kill plants if there are so many in an area that they can't get enough sunlight. And nitrogen fertilizers run off into lakes, causing algae and water plants to grow too quickly. They may use up so much oxygen as they die and decay that there is no longer enough to support fish and other creatures.

Nitrogen can harm the environment in yet another way. In the last few decades, very large quantities of nitrogen oxides have been given off by power plants and cars. When these pollutants mix with water particles in the air, they fall back to Earth as *acid rain*. In some places, this rain contains so much nitric acid that it eats away statues. When the rainwater runs off into lakes, it can kill fish and other water creatures. The water may even become too acidic for us to drink.

If people cut down on pollution, the amount of acid rain will lessen. But to correct the imbalance in the nitrogen cycle, we must greatly reduce ammonia production. Some farmers have begun using manure instead of manufactured fertilizers because they believe that vegetables fertilized naturally are healthier to eat. If less fertilizer is manufactured as a result, this method of farming could help balance the nitrogen cycle.

Fortunately, we are in no danger of running out of nitrogen in the air any time soon. Even if the imbalance in the nitrogen cycle continues, it will take millions of years for all the nitrogen in the air to disappear.

Once you understand the nitrogen cycle, you will begin to see that death and decay are just as important to the health of our world as life and growth. Life is amazing and wonderful, yet we must not forget that death is necessary to create it.

Nitrogen fertilizers can pollute lakes, like this one in Minnesota, by increasing the growth of algae and other plants.

Glossary

acid—a sour-tasting compound that reacts with bases, or alkalis, to form salt compounds.

acid rain—rain containing an acid as a result of polluting gases, such as nitrogen dioxide. The pollution is caused by cars and industries.

amine group—an NH_2 group that attached to a compound.

amino acids—compounds containing chains of carbon atoms with NH_2 groups, oxygen, and sometimes sulfur attached. They are the building blocks of proteins.

atom—the smallest piece of an element. Each element has an atom with a unique number of protons and electrons.

atomic number—the number of protons in the atom of an element. This number identifies the element, since each element has a different number of protons.

azote—a name Antoine Lavoisier gave to nitrogen in 1789. In Greek, it means "no life."

carbon—an element with six protons and electrons. Charcoal is one form of carbon.

carbon dioxide—an invisible gas that animals exhale and plants absorb. It is a compound of carbon and oxygen (CO_2).

catalyst—a substance that speeds up a chemical reaction.

chemical reaction—a process in which substances combine or decompose to form different substances. In other words, atoms bond together to form compounds or break apart into elements.

compound—a substance made up of two or more elements chemically bonded together.

coordinate bond—an unusual bond that nitrogen often makes with other elements.

corrosion—a process in which metals wear away because of a chemical reaction with oxygen and water.

double bond—a bond in which each atom shares two electrons.

dynamite—an explosive containing a material soaked in nitroglycerin.

electron—a tiny particle that moves around the nucleus of an atom and has a negative electric charge. Electricity is a flow of electrons.

element—a basic substance that cannot be broken down into any simpler substance. There are ninety-two elements in nature, and about twenty more have been generated artificially.

enzyme—a substance that aids chemical reactions in the body.

fire air—an eighteenth-century term for oxygen.

foul air—an eighteenth-century term for nitrogen.

gas—a substance that has no definite shape or volume, but spreads into whatever space is available. It is the form a substance takes when the temperature of its liquid form is raised so high that its molecules rise into the air. The "gas" people put in their cars is different; it is short for the liquid gasoline.

hydrogen—the lightest in weight of all the elements. It is an invisible gas that burns in oxygen to produce water.

molecule—a group of two or more atoms bonded together to form a compound. They sometimes form in elements too, especially gases, as atom pairs.

niter—a saltlike compound containing nitrogen, with the chemical name potassium nitrate (KNO_3). It is also known as saltpeter.

nitrates—compounds containing NO_3 as part of their formulas.

nitric acid—a strong acid with the formula HNO_3.

nitric oxide—an invisible, poisonous gas that forms when electricity or lightning, which is natural electricity, passes through nitrogen and oxygen gases. Its formula is NO.

nitrogen—an invisible gas that accounts for about four-fifths of the air. In Greek, it means "generator of niter."

nitrogen cycle—the process in which nitrogen moves from the air to the earth and back again through decay. In the soil, the nitrogen fertilizes plants, and the plants feed animals.

nitrogen dioxide—a reddish-brown poisonous gas that forms when oxygen is mixed with nitric oxide. Its formula is NO_2.

nitrogen fixation—a breaking of the bond between the two atoms in a molecule of nitrogen gas, making the atoms available for bonding with other elements.

nitrogen oxide—compounds of nitrogen and oxygen. They include nitric oxide (NO), nitrogen dioxide (NO_2), nitrous oxide (N_2O), nitrogen trioxide (N_2O_3), and nitrogen pentoxide (N_2O_5).

nitroglycerin—an oily liquid that can explode or, in tiny amounts, cause blood vessels to enlarge. Its formula is $C_3H_5N_3O_9$.

nitrous oxide—an invisible gas, also known as laughing gas, that can act as an anesthetic when it is inhaled. Its formula is N_2O.

nucleus—the center of an atom, where the protons are located.

potassium—a white, powdery metal, an element found in many minerals.

protein—the building material of plants and animals. Different types of proteins also control and carry out body functions. They are made of amino acids, which contain nitrogen as the most important element.

proton—a particle in the center, or nucleus, of an atom. It has a positive electric charge. The number of protons in an atom determines which element it is.

root nodule—a swelling on the root of a plant that contains nitrogen-fixing bacteria.

saltpeter—another name for niter, potassium nitrate (KNO_3). Chile saltpeter is a similar compound found as a mineral in Chile—sodium nitrate ($NaNO_3$).

TNT—a powerful military explosive made of the compound trinitrotoluene ($C_7H_5N_3O_6$).

triple bond—a bond in which each atom shares three electrons.

urea—the main compound in human urine that results from the decay of proteins. Its formula is $C_2O(NH_2)_2$.

Sources

Brock, William H. *The Norton History of Chemistry*. New York: Norton, 1992.

Dictionary of Scientific Biography. New York: Scribner, 1970–80.

Farber, Eduard. *Great Chemists*. New York: Interscience, 1961.

Greenwood, N.N., and A. Earnshaw. *Chemistry of the Elements*. Oxford, England: Pergamon Press, 1984.

Hudson, John. *The History of Chemistry*. New York: Routledge, Chapman, & Hall, 1992.

Newton, David E. *The Chemical Elements*. New York: Franklin Watts, 1994.

Partington, J. R. *A History of Chemistry*. London: Macmillan, 1962.

Postgate, John. *Biological Nitrogen Fixation*. Watford Herts, England: Merrow Publishing, 1972.

Sittig, Marshall. *Nitrogen in Industry*. Princeton, NJ: Van Nostrand, 1965.

Weeks, Mary Elvira. *Discovery of the Elements*. Easton, PA: Journal of Chemical Education, 1968.

Index

61

About the Author

Karen Fitzgerald is a science writer and former Franklin Watts editor. She has also worked as an editor for *The Sciences*, a magazine published by the New York Academy of Sciences, and *Spectrum*, a technology magazine published by the Institute of Electrical and Electronics Engineers. She has written articles for magazines including *Scientific American*, *Omni*, and *Science World*. Her bachelor's degree is in mechanical engineering from the University of Illinois in Urbana, and she has a master's degree in science and environmental reporting from New York University.